The field mouse has sandy brown fur and a white belly and a long tail. It has big back feet that are like a spring when it leaps. It eats seeds, but it also eats snails, insects, nuts and berries.

The main predators of mice are cats, wild dogs, foxes, owls and other kinds of birds of prey, skunks and snakes.

You can find mice all over the world, except in Antarctica. There are more than 30 different types of mice. A baby mouse is called a 'pinky', a male is called a 'buck' and a female is called a 'doe'. Dormice are not true mice, but they make a sweet pet.

Mice are nocturnal animals. They are not blind, but their sight is not the best! They have a great sense of hearing and smell, and they use their whiskers to help feel their way.

Mice are very nimble animals and can run very fast. They are also great at climbing and can swim! In the wild, they thrive in forests and grasslands, but they also live in houses!

The house mouse is very common. It has a brown-grey shiny coat, big eyes and ears and a pointed snout. Its tail is as long as its body. Mice are great pets – they don't bite, but they can be quite smelly!

Mice are clean, tidy animals and like to groom themselves several times a day. In the wild, mice build complex burrows with different spaces for sleeping, keeping their food, and going to the loo!

Fun fact: House mice eat 15 to 20 times a day. But despite what you might think, they don't like cheese. They prefer cereals.... or chocolate!